Cities through Time

Daily Life in Ancient and Modern

TIMBUKTU

by Larry Brook

illustrations by Ray Webb

Ꝛ₱

Runestone Press/Minneapolis
A Division of the Lerner Publishing Group

The *Cities through Time* series is produced by Runestone Press, a division of the Lerner Publishing Group, in cooperation with Greenleaf Publishing, Inc., Geneva, Illinois.

Text designed by Melanie Lawson
Cover designed by Michael Tacheny

The Lerner Publishing Group
241 First Avenue North
Minneapolis, Minnesota 55401

Website address: www.lernerbooks.com

The modern, official spelling of Timbuktu is Tombouctou. For ease of recognition, the more traditional spelling has been adopted for this book. A guide for hard-to-pronounce words can be found on page 61.

Library of Congress Cataloging-in-Publication Data

Brook, Larry
    Daily life in ancient and modern Timbuktu / by Larry Brook ; illustrations by Ray Webb.
        p. cm. — (Cities through time)
    Includes bibliographical references and index.
    Summary: Examines the history of the city of Timbuktu, or Tombouctou, from its time as a camping site for nomadic Tuaregs through its prominence in the sixteenth century to the current decline it faces.
    ISBN: 0–8225–3215–8 (lib. bdg. : alk. paper)
    1. Tombouctou (Mali)—Social life and customs—Juvenile literature. [1. Tombouctou (Mali)] I. Webb, Ray, ill.
    II. Title. III. Series.
    DT551.9.T55B76 1999
    966.23—dc21   98–18314

Manufactured in the United States of America
1 2 3 4 5 6 – JR – 04 03 02 01 00 99

Contents

Introduction

Fabled Timbuktu clings to the edge of the Sahara Desert. The city lies in the Sahel (the southern edge of the Sahara), eight miles north of the Niger River in the West African nation of Mali. Two-story mud-brick houses crowd narrow streets filled with ankle-deep sand. Only a few structures—a couple of hotels and the minarets of old mosques (Islamic houses of prayer)—rise into the pale blue sky. A visitor can walk from one end of Timbuktu to the other in less than 20 minutes. The city's small population of just over 20,000 come from a rich ethnic background that has both Arab and black African roots.

Four hundred years ago, however, Timbuktu was a thriving metropolis of more than 100,000 people, with two universities, 180 schools, and more than 20,000 scholars. From a small campground along the banks of the Niger River, Timbuktu had grown to become known as the "Pearl of Africa."

In the late 1500s, armies from Morocco, northwest of Mali, overran Timbuktu, beginning its long decline. This decline was hastened when ancient caravan routes, the chief source of Timbuktu's income and place in history, began shifting eastward.

From the sixteenth to the nineteenth centuries, more than 40 European explorers searched for Timbuktu. They were tantalized by legends of gold nuggets the size of peaches said to be scattered on the river bottoms. Finally, in 1894, French gunboats sailed up the Niger and colonized the city along with the rest of the area that would become Mali.

Mali gained independence from France in 1960. Drought and famine hit the region in the 1970s, and thousands of people and livestock died. The city has also suffered from war between roving fighters and the national armies of Mali, Burkina Faso, Mauritania, and Niger. One official in Bamako, Mali's capital, remains hopeful. Economic development, he said, will work miracles in Timbuktu. "All we need is some peace and stability."

4

On the Banks of the Niger

*T*imbuktu lies near a wide turn of the Niger River. The mighty waterway flows northeastward out of the raised plateaus of Guinea, goes through the sands of the Sahara for hundreds of miles, and then curves southward to empty into the Gulf of Guinea on the coast of Nigeria.

Because of the seasonal rise and fall of the Niger River, some cities along its banks, such as Djenné, frequently experience floods. Timbuktu, roughly eight

miles north of the river, remains dry. In addition, upon nearing Timbuktu, the river begins its eastward arc, forming a natural port at the village of Kabara, which sits in the channel itself. At high tide, the Niger fills a low area that cuts all the way to Timbuktu. In the past, pirogues (wooden canoes) could reach the city directly. At other times, traders hauled their goods to the city on the backs of donkeys.

Timbuktu's location lured merchants from other towns, such as nearby Walata (in modern-day Mauritania). Empires rose and fell around Timbuktu, each contributing to its riches, culture, and religion. At one time, the city was wealthier than Paris, London, or Rome.

In this nineteenth-century painting, a caravan waits along the shore of the Niger River for a trading ship.

A mat divided Tuareg tents down the middle. One side was for the women, and the other for the men.

A Seasonal Encampment

The first recorded mention of Timbuktu is in the Arabic chronicles of Abd al-Rahman al-Sadi, a writer who lived all his life in Timbuktu. Al-Sadi wrote that in the early 1100s, Timbuktu was merely a seasonal camp on the Niger River, where "travelers arriving by land and water met." In the early days, the main travelers to Timbuktu were the Tuareg, a nomadic people related to the Berbers of North Africa. They made an annual journey between Arawan, to the north, and Lake Debo on the Niger.

These nomads, al-Sadi explains, "made [Timbuktu] a depot for their utensils and their grain. Soon it became a crossroads of travelers who passed back and forth through it." They entrusted their property to a slave woman called Buctoo. The Tuareg word *tim*, meaning "that belongs to," and the woman's name were combined to make the city's name.

The Tuareg

In ancient Timbuktu, the Tuareg offered tea, their greatest luxury, to guests of honor. Special guests were seated in front of the tent on straw mats. The arrival of newcomers prompted a celebration because guests were so few and far between in the huge expanse of the desert. Following a ritual of bowing and smiling, the host gathered his robes about him and sat, followed by the guests. The tea, a thick, sweet mixture, was offered in tiny cups, usually in three servings. The first cup was strong to cut the harsh taste of the desert. The second cup was sweet to give love, and the third was weak to add pleasure. Conversation was elaborate and

Tuareg men wore veils, even when inside their tents. The veils, dyed with dark indigo, left blue stains on their faces. The stains gave Tuareg males the nickname the "blue men."

polite, in keeping with the dignity of the desert. The Tuareg extended this courtesy to strangers because someday the host, too, might be in need. A minor error in navigation while searching for an oasis (fertile area) could end in death. Even entire caravans were not safe from danger. In one case, 2,000 travelers and 1,800 camels, carrying salt between Taou-denni (an oasis in northern Mali) and Timbuktu, lost their way and died. The Tuareg determined the time to head north by the seasons. The rainy season lasted from June to October. Then came the summer sandstorm season between October and June, when the daytime temperature could reach 130°F, and the nights were below freezing.

Remain Calm

The Tuareg enjoyed the open spaces and freedom of the desert, which they knew well. They could identify where they were by the shape of specific hills and by the feel, color, and taste of the sand. At night, they navigated by the stars. An ancient Tuareg saying was, "If you get lost, remain calm for the desert is calm."

Nomads of the Sand

Days for Tuareg men began at sunrise, whether they were resting at Timbuktu or trekking through the desert. After feeding and milking the camels and goats, they went to their tents for breakfast.

The men were responsible for keeping the family and the livestock alive. They searched constantly for water, following the rains, moving from oasis to oasis.

Even when there was rain, desert vegetation for grazing was scarce. Boys took up the work of herding and caring for the camels at age 10 and were hardened early to the demands of survival. Sometimes a camel would wander off, and a young herder would go after it, only to lose his bearings. Months later his skeleton would be found in the sand.

When different Tuareg clans met, the men would hold camel races. At night the men sat outside in the cool air and talked business, told stories, or sang songs. Sometimes, as the women played drums and sang, the men danced with the camels, moving them to the beat.

This nineteenth-century painting depicts a camel caravan similar to those formed by the Tuareg.

12

Know Your Camel

Boys had to learn to recognize the brands burned into each camel as well as each animal's tracks. With practice, by looking at a camel's tracks, boys could tell the camel's sex and how long ago the footprint was made. As they grew older, the boys would be able to pick out their own camels from thousands of others.

Women of the Desert

Tuareg women rose at dawn, usually when their husbands brought them a bowl of goat milk, which they shared with the children. The women and girls cooked all of the food inside the tent. They prepared yogurt, butter, cheese, goat meat, milk, dates, and *tagila*, a flat whole wheat bread. They also ground wheat to make couscous, a steamed, ricelike dish mixed with meat or fruit. It was said that a girl was old enough to learn to cook when she could stir a small stick in the couscous.

Tuareg women dyed their own cloth and made their own clothes. They taught their daughters to weave baskets for storing food and cradling babies. Women also bartered for grain and vegetables from other nomads and later, when Timbuktu became a town, from merchants in the market.

When Tuareg nomads arrived in Timbuktu, the entire family helped set up camp. While the men and boys unloaded the camels, women and girls unraveled the woven grass or camelskin tents fringed with green, red, and blue leather. The females spaced the tents widely because Tuareg families valued their privacy. After the tents were set up, the men tended the herds, while the women hung food from tripods or stored it in calabashes (bowls made of dried gourds), in trees, or in separate food tents. When it came time to depart, women did the packing. They rolled up the tents, blankets, and food. Girls packed the calabashes into leather saddlebags. Their job was to be sure the *guerbas* (goatskin tanks) were filled with water and covered tightly. It could be a matter of life or death if a guerba leaked even a little bit on journeys.

Women were highly respected in ancient Timbuktu and took part in all major decisions. If a woman divorced her husband, she took the tent with her. Sometimes a woman owned more property, sheep, goats, and camels than her husband did.

The Arrival of Islam

Muhammad, the founder of the Islamic religion, was born in about A.D. 570 on the Arabian Peninsula. In 640, eight years after his death, Islamic armies crossed into North Africa, where Christianity had earlier taken hold. During the next 60 years, Islam replaced Christianity throughout the region.

By the eighth and ninth centuries, most merchants in the trans-Saharan trade were Muslims (followers of Islam). They helped to bring Islam to Timbuktu. The religion intrigued the city's residents. They were attracted to the Muslim practice that allowed each man to have as many wives (up to four) as he could support. Most of the local inhabitants had never seen paper with writing, so they thought the Koran, the Islamic holy book, was magic. By 1336 most of Timbuktu's people were Muslims.

In Timbuktu teachers called *mirabouts* started schools where the main subject was Arabic, the language in which the Koran was written. In the early years, Islamic education was stern. Ibn Battutah, a Moroccan writer who traveled to Timbuktu in the mid-1300s, explained, "They put their children in chains if they showed backwardness in memorizing the Koran." Eventually, Timbuktu became a great center of Islamic learning, and several mosques were constructed.

Boys in Timbuktu attended classes where the Koran was studied. The teachers insisted that students memorize large portions of the holy book.

A City of Learning

Salt comes from the north, gold from the south, but pious and learned things and pretty stories we find nowhere but in Timbuctoo. —local proverb

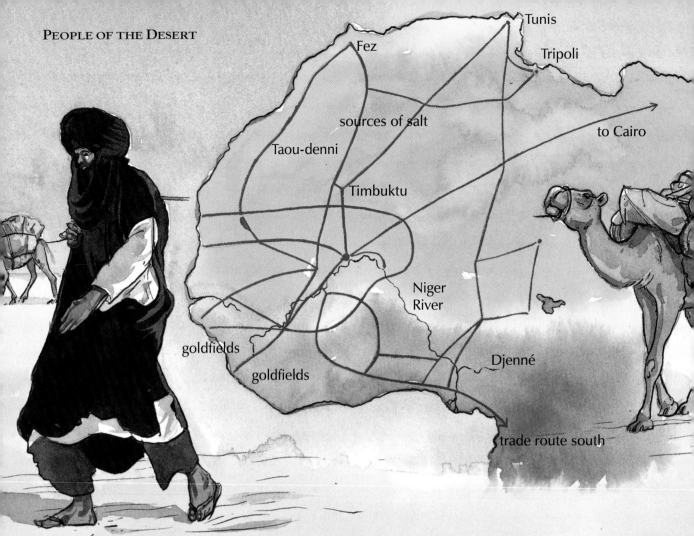

Tunis

Fez

Tripoli

sources of salt

to Cairo

Taou-denni

Timbuktu

Niger
River

goldfields

Djenné

goldfields

trade route south

Salt and Gold

The Islamic faith and the Arabic language unified North Africa, and trade routes expanded quickly. By the fourteenth century, caravans of up to 50,000 camels moved south toward Timbuktu, carrying slabs of salt, delicately carved daggers, timepieces, silks, beads, jewelry, and fine cloth.

Returning north to the desert, the merchants carried gold from Ghana and Guinea, where miners dug 50-foot shafts to extract the metal. The traders also brought leather, cotton, kola nuts, pots of shea butter (the fatty fruit from nut trees), baskets of grains like millet and sorghum, bars of iron, and slaves.

The primary exchange, though, was gold for salt and salt for gold. Desert peoples were desperate for salt because it couldn't be mined locally. The Italian

Salt Coins

When the value of salt soared to that of gold, salt vendors were careful never to waste their wares, saving even the smallest remainders for sale. Salt was even used as currency in some regions. Cut into nine-inch cylinders, it was lightweight and easy to carry.

traveler, Alvise da Ca da Mosto, writing in the 1400s, underlined the need for salt, "At the season of the year of the great heats, their blood . . . putrefies. And if it were not for salt they would die."

Salt from Taou-denni in the Sahara was white and dense. Slaves or prisoners cut the rock salt out of stratified beds and carved them into the shape of tombstones, each weighing more than 50 pounds. Timbuktu was a hive of activity as men loaded the bars of salt onto pirogues at the outskirts of town and floated them southward into the Niger River. The eventual destination of the salt was Djenné. There porters loaded the salt slabs on their heads and carried them south to the gold mines. The ancient historian, al-Sadi, wrote, "Djenné is one of the greatest Muslim markets where traders with salt . . . meet traders with gold. . . . It is because of this blessed town [Djenné] that caravans come to Timbuktu from all points of the horizon."

Trade brought wealth to Timbuktu.

The Mali Empire

The Ghana Empire, crumbled in 1076, when its capital city of Kumbi Saleh was captured and sacked by a fierce army of desert people called Almoravids. At this time, Timbuktu was still an obscure Tuareg watering hole.

The Mali Empire, which surpassed the empire of Ghana in power and wealth, arose in the 1200s and had a profound impact on the growth of Timbuktu. The empire began as a small kingdom of Malinke people in Kangaba (near the modern border between Mali and Guinea). Independent for a time, Kangaba was eventually conquered by the Sosso people.

The Sosso conqueror was King Sumanguru. To gain his objective, he assassinated 11 of his brothers, all heirs to the Kangaba throne. Sumanguru made the fatal mistake of sparing the life of the twelfth brother, Sundiata. Sundiata, whose name means "hungering lion" in Malinke, fled. While in exile, he learned to hunt, ride a horse, and lead an army. Sundiata defeated Sumanguru in the famous Battle of Kirina in 1235 and began building what would become the Mali Empire.

He made Niani (in modern Guinea) on the Niger River his capital. This shift contributed directly to the rapid development of Timbuktu. The city became not only a key trading hub but also a center of Islamic learning.

Sundiata's son Mansa Uli gained control of Timbuktu and Djenné. Eventually, Mali grew to be three times the size of the Ghana Empire, covering present-day Gambia, Guinea, Mali, Senegal, and portions of Burkina Faso, Mauritania, and Niger. Sundiata's descendants ruled this vast domain for more than 200 years.

Growing Up in Mali

Malinke life centered around the group's children, who were in the care of their mothers during the first 12 years of life. When boys reached 12, they were apprenticed to their uncles to learn a trade. If the family was wealthy, they would send their boy to Timbuktu to learn from a master craftsperson.

Weavers and blacksmiths were the most valued artisans. Apprenticeships with them were the most sought after. The weaver's work was filled with symbols. Even a weaver's eight-part loom had meaning. For example, four parts of the weaver's frame stood for the chief elements—earth, air, fire, and water. The other four stood for north, south, east, and west. Before beginning work, the weaver prayed over the loom, touching each part.

Although young girls were cherished, they were not allowed to study or learn a trade. When a girl turned 13 or 14, she was ready for marriage. An exchange of kola nuts marked the beginning of negotiations between a groom and his in-laws. The father of the bride paid a bride-price, perhaps some sheep or a few horses. On the wedding day, older women took care of the bride, braiding her hair and oiling and perfuming her body. At sunset the procession formed in front of the groom's aunt's house. The bride came out, surrounded by her family and a choir singing a departure song. The groom greeted the bride and offered her a necklace or bracelet that he'd made. Then he welcomed the bride into her new house. Family and friends danced and sang in front of the house until the groom's uncle gave them gifts and sent them away. The farewell signified the ceremony was complete.

The Malinke had many instruments. The *tabala* was a ceremonial drum. The *guimbris* was a two-stringed guitar. For war musicians played the three-stringed *bolon*. For pleasure they played the *kora*, a 27-stringed harp, and the *balaphon*, a xylophone made of blocks of wood placed over gourds.

23

A Visitor to Mali

The garments of [Timbuktu's] inhabitants . . . are of fine Egyptian fabrics. [Its] women are of surpassing beauty and are shown more respect than the men. The state of affairs among these people is indeed extraordinary. These people are Muslims, . . . observing the hours of prayer, studying books of law, and memorizing the Koran. Yet their women show no bashfulness before men and do not veil themselves.

—Moroccan traveler, Ibn Battutah

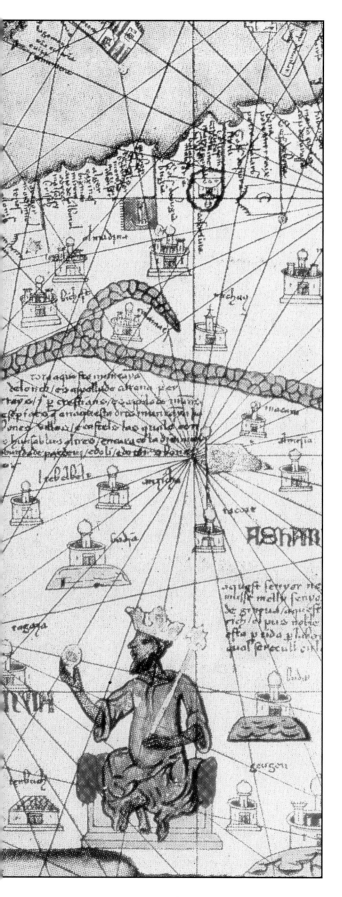

Mansa Musa

Mansa Musa was the grandson of Sundiata's sister. Between 1312 and about 1332, he built Mali into a large, strong, and prosperous empire. With his huge army, Mansa Musa defeated the Tuareg and expanded trade. He boasted that it would take one year to travel across his kingdom from west to east.

Mansa Musa did more than anyone to establish Timbuktu's reputation as a legendary "city of gold." In 1324 he staged a lavish 6,000-mile roundtrip to Mecca, an Islamic holy city on the Arabian Peninsula. Witnesses reported that during the trek across the Sahara he wore embroidered silk robes. His 60,000 escorts included his senior wife Inari-Kunate and her 500 maids and slaves. One hundred camels, each carrying 300 pounds of gold, also came along.

When he reached the Egyptian city of Cairo, Mansa Musa distributed gold—1,000 raw ingots to the emir (ruler) and a large sum to every officer of the court. He gave out so much gold that the value of money on the Cairo market was ruined for a decade.

Abraham Cresques, a fourteenth-century mapmaker living in Spain, completed the Catalan atlas in 1375. In it he describes Mansa Musa (on throne, lower right) as "the richest and most noble king in all the land."

Palace and Mosque

Upon his return from Mecca in 1330, Mansa Musa brought many scholars with him, as well as the gifted poet and architect, Abu Ishaq al-Saheli of Spain. Al-Saheli built Timbuktu's famous Djinguereber mosque, one of the oldest mosques in West Africa, and Mansa Musa's palace. Leo Africanus, a visitor to Timbuktu 200 years later, described the mosque and the palace: "There is a most stately temple to be seen, the walls whereof are made of stone and lime; and a princely palace also built by a most excellent workman of [the Spanish city of] Granada."

26

Arms of Gold

Mansa Musa holds court in his palace on a great balcony called a bembe *where he has a great seat of ebony that is like a throne. On either side it is flanked by elephant tusks. His arms stand near him, being all of gold—saber, lance, quiver, bow, and arrows.*

—Al-Umari, a historian of the time

Storms sometimes filled the streets of Timbuktu with sand, eventually causing the streets to be higher than the floors of the houses. The same types of buildings and walls still remain *(below)*.

Houses of Mud

Al-Saheli's architecture changed the way buildings were constructed in the climatic conditions of Timbuktu. Before his arrival, the houses tended to be round with cone roofs. Al-Saheli introduced square houses with flat roofs. To cope with heavy rains that often washed away the mud walls, he inserted wooden posts into the outside walls. These provided sturdy support against the rains as well as a scaffolding to climb on when repairs were needed.

The walls of the houses were built of bricks made by hand out of desert sand and clay with garbage thrown in for binding. Roofs had drains made of split palm trunks. The few windows were small and high up. Doors were elaborately constructed of wood, with large rings as knockers. By the end of the sixteenth century, the doors also had wooden grills imported from Morocco.

The inside rooms were narrow and dark with dirt floors. They were narrow because the beams were made of split palm trunks, cut short. Palm fronds and matting were laid over the beams and plastered with mud to make a second story or the roof. The ground floor usually opened into a small enclosed courtyard, where the cooking was done. A wicker bed and a thin mattress of rushes or reed mats with leather cushions were the only furniture. Some houses had low benches made of mud jutting out into the street on either side of the front door. This was where the men liked to spread out their mats and sleep outside where it is cooler.

One of the earliest published drawings of Timbuktu

Rise of the Songhai Empire

Not long after Mansa Musa's death, warriors from around the Volta River attacked Timbuktu and burned parts of the city to the ground. The event shocked the Mali Empire, and throughout the next century its power declined. In 1433 Tuareg raiders seized control of Timbuktu and rebuilt it.

Meanwhile, the small Songhai kingdom was on the rise. One of its rulers was Sonni Ali, or Ali the Great, who took the throne in 1464. Using his skilled army, Ali crushed nomadic raiders, captured large caravans, and extended Songhai authority into the old Mali territory.

Timbuktu soon drew Sonni Ali's attention. The city was once again a bustling crossroads of trade. Its universities attracted students and scholars from throughout the Islamic world.

However, a Tuareg chief controlled Timbuktu. Sonni Ali decided to conquer the city. He sent so huge an army that when it came close to the city, the cavalry's horses kicked up great clouds of dust. Sonni Ali marched into Timbuktu, unopposed, in ranks of soldiers and horses. The sight of this vast army sent the Tuareg chief fleeing into the desert.

Although they had chafed under Tuareg rule, Timbuktu's Islamic students and scholars were in a panic. For years they had ridiculed the Songhai as ignorant and considered their king a Muslim in name only. Sonni Ali took his revenge. He sacked the city and killed thousands of Islamic leaders, chasing the rest into the desert. Al-Sadi called Sonni Ali "the tyrant, the accursed, scoundrel, unjust, bloody, who caused the death of so many that Allah alone can count them." But Sonni Ali prevailed, and by the time of his death in 1492, he had built Songhai into a formidable empire.

The Glory of Timbuktu

Timbuktu reached its peak of power and influence under the Songhai ruler Askia Muhammad. Muhammad Touré, his real name, was a soldier when he overthrew Sonni Ali's son to gain control of the empire. He then took on the title Askia, or general. He was not only a brilliant general and administrator but also a devout Muslim. His fame attracted many more students and scholars to Timbuktu, whose population soon rose to 100,000. Askia Muhammad's power eventually extended all the way to the Atlantic Ocean, bringing peace, learning, and fabulous wealth to his subjects.

At the height of Askia Muhammad's reign, in 1510, Leo Africanus, an Arab born in Spain, visited Timbuktu. He was impressed by what he saw: "Whosoever will speak unto the king must first fall down before his feet, and then taking up earth must sprinkle it upon his own head and shoulders. He hath always three thousand horsemen and a great number of footmen that shoot poisoned arrows."

After making a tour of the city, Leo Africanus wrote, "Here are a great store of doctors, judges, priests, and other learned men that are bountifully maintained at the king's cost and charges. And hither are brought diverse books, which are sold for more money than any other merchandise." He was surprised at the wealth of the people and envied their many wells "containing most sweet water."

But it wasn't only the wealth and advanced culture that impressed him. He genuinely liked the residents of Timbuktu. "The inhabitants are people of a gentle and cheerful disposition," he said, "and spend a great part of the night in singing and dancing through all the streets of the city."

The Muslim faithful, who often pray at mosques *(right),* are required by the Koran *(below)* to follow five rules.

1. Believe that there is no God but Allah and that Muhammad is his prophet.

2. Pray five times a day—at dawn, noon, midafternoon, sunset, and nightfall.

3. Give to the needy.

4. Fast during Ramadan, the ninth month of the year, from sunup to sundown.

5. Once in a lifetime, make a pilgrimage, called the hajj, to the holy city of Mecca.

Slave Life

African societies had practiced slavery as early as 1000 B.C. They sold slaves to one another and exported them to North Africa and Asia. Slaves were in high demand in the Sahara. Arab merchants used them as porters to cross the desert. Ibn Battutah reported that he once saw a caravan crossing the Sahara with more than 10,000 slaves.

Slaves had always been a part of the daily life in Timbuktu, not only during the days of the Songhai Empire, but even earlier, under the Tuareg and during the era of the Mali Empire. They were brought to Timbuktu and sold for horses, spices, cloth, and sometimes weapons.

In Songhai society, slaves could purchase their freedom. Some slaveholders gave their slaves lifelong positions that offered a measure of independence. Askia Muhammad, for instance, was given two dozen slave families who each owed him a special service. The members of one family were royal bodyguards or ladies in waiting in the royal household. Five of the families manufactured weapons—100 spears and 100 arrows with metal tips per year. River families were required to give the emperor dried fish and to operate canoes. Another family of slaves was assigned to farm the land and to harvest crops to feed the emperor's horses.

Slaves were captives of war, prisoners of raiding expeditions, criminals, or enemies of the state. They were captured by slave traders.

In the African Empires of the Middle Ages, slavery was an accepted institution. . . . But there is no evidence of plantation slavery, at least in sub-Saharan Africa, until Europeans came on the scene [in the late 1400s].
—L. H. Ofosu-Appiah

Morocco Invades

Timbuktu's prosperity was not to last. In 1591 Moroccan soldiers and troops for hire invaded the Songhai Empire. The sultan (ruler) of Morocco was obsessed with taking over Songhai's lucrative salt and gold trade. To achieve this end, he chose as general Judar Pasha, a young Spaniard with no military experience. Judar Pasha led an army of 4,000 soldiers and 10,000 camels across 1,700 miles of desert. Five months later, when they finally reached Timbuktu, only 1,000 soldiers remained.

But equipped with cannons and with harquebuses—the most modern rifles of the day—they were strong enough to defeat the Songhai army of 9,700 infantry armed with bows and arrows and 18,000 cavalry with spears. Timbuktu fell quickly.

Mahmud Pasha was eventually appointed to replace the weary Judar Pasha. While under Moroccan occupation, Mahmud announced there would be a house-to-house search for weapons. But the announcement was a deception. The newcomers said they would not come near the houses of those who were descendants of a certain Islamic holy man. Overnight, residents carried their valuables to the houses of these descendants, trusting that they would be safe. The next day, the conquerors called the male descendants to prayer. As soon as the doors of the mosque were shut, troops went to their houses, stole the treasures of Timbuktu, and then massacred most of the men in the mosque.

With further battles, the order and discipline of the Songhai administration dissolved. The once-peaceful empire became a group of local city-states that warred with one another off and on for the next 300 years.

At about the same time, European merchant ships began sailing down the western coast of Africa. They found a new way to West African markets and no longer needed to depend on the caravan trade routes across the Sahara. Timbuktu lost its basis for wealth.

Military rule upset the scholastic and spiritual focus of Timbuktu.
Morrocan soldiers terrorized the city's scholars, most of whom had
never defended themselves physically.

Searching for the Fabled Golden City

The people of Europe knew nothing of the decline of Timbuktu. Most still believed in a legendary city of gold, and dozens of explorers lost their lives searching for it.

Among these was Mungo Park, a Scottish explorer. In 1805, after a disastrous expedition in which more than 30 men died, Park reached the port of Timbuktu. Tuareg fighters attacked Park and his remaining crew, killing them or causing them to drown in the Niger's fierce currents.

Major Alexander Gordon Laing, another explorer from Scotland, crossed the Sahara with an Arab caravan. Not far from Timbuktu, the Tuareg ambushed him. Laing received a gunshot wound, deep sword slashes all over his body, and a broken jaw. The attackers cut off a piece of his ear and nearly severed his right hand. Arab friends carried him to Timbuktu on August 18, 1826, where he amazingly recovered. However, on September 26, 1826, as he was leaving Timbuktu with another caravan, he was again attacked by the Tuareg. This time, they strangled him to death and burned all his travel notes.

This view of Timbuktu was sketched by Heinrich Barth, another early visitor to Timbuktu. Mungo Park (*inset*) was the first European to discover that the Niger River flowed eastward.

A Lost City Rediscovered

The harrowing events of the Europeans only sparked more interest in the region. In 1824 the French geographic society came up with an amazing offer. A prize of 10,000 francs would go to anyone who could reach Timbuktu and return safely.

A young Frenchman, René-Auguste Caillié, took up the challenge. Disguising himself as a Muslim, he joined a caravan in March 1827 that reached Timbuktu a year later. When he saw the city for the first time at sunset, he wrote in his journal of his feeling of "indescribable satisfaction."

Waking up the next day, he was disappointed. Instead of a city of gold, he saw, "a mass of ill-looking houses, built of earth. Nothing was to be seen in all directions but immense plains of quicksand of a yellowish white color," he wrote. "The most profound silence prevailed; not even the warbling of a bird was to be heard. Still, there was something imposing in the aspect of a great city, raised in the midst of sands, and the difficulties surmounted by its founders cannot fail to excite admiration."

Caillié stayed in Timbuktu for two weeks and then left cautiously—again in disguise—with a large caravan of 400 Arabs and 1,400 camels. Two months later, he arrived in France and was given the cash prize. He later wrote *Travels through Central Africa to Timbuctoo,* a two-volume work about his adventures.

Caillié is shown *(right, in hat)* crossing a river on his way to Timbuktu. This engraving depicts him traveling in European dress. In fact, he had to disguise himself in native costume to enter the city.

Caillié's Journal

First meal: *"[My host] invited me to sup with him; and an excellent couscous of millet and mutton was served up. Six of us partook of the dish, and we ate with our fingers."*

A walk through the city: *"The streets are clean, and sufficiently wide to permit three horsemen to pass abreast. The city is situated in an immense plain of white sand, having no vegetation but stunted trees and shrubs. The city is not closed by any barrier and may be entered on any side. In the center is a palm tree. I was surprised at the inactivity. Some kola-nut vendors were crying their goods in the streets."*

Slaves: *"A few days after I arrived in Timbuctoo, I saw two [slave] women. They wore fine white [dresses], large gold earrings, and each had two or three necklaces. When I passed them they looked at me and smiled. They did not appear in the least mortified at being exhibited in the streets for sale. In general, the slaves are better treated at Timbuctoo than in other countries."*

The great mosque: *"I visited the great mosque on the west side of town. The walls are in bad repair, their facing being damaged by rain. Several buttresses are raised against the wall to support them. I ascended the tower, though its staircase is almost demolished."*

Market Day

Market day in Timbuktu in the early 1800s was much the same as it had been for centuries. To avoid the heat, merchants didn't gather until around three in the afternoon. Then they set up stalls covered with mats to protect them against the heat of the sun.

Salt was the most important item for sale in Timbuktu. Large caravans, with camels laden with salt slabs from Taou-denni, entered the city. From nearby Djenné, merchants brought in everything else their buyers might need. These goods included goat meat, millet, rice, vegetable butter, honey, cotton, cloth, preserved provisions, candles, soap, allspice, onions, dried fish, pistachios, and so on.

A merchant might also sell something special, perhaps elephants' tusks obtained from the Tuareg, who snared rather than shot the huge animals. Merchants also displayed articles from Europe, such as glassware, amber, coral, sulfur, paper, double-barreled guns, and French muskets.

This nineteenth-century painting shows a toy seller spreading out his handcrafted toy birds.

42

French Gunboats

*I*n the decades following Caillié's visit to Timbuktu, local commanders—such as Al-Hajj Umar, Ahmadu Tall, and Samory Touré—sought to subdue the land that the Mali and Songhai Empires had once controlled. But in time these leaders would be crushed by the French, who were creating an altogether new empire in Africa.

The French already controlled much of West Africa, but in the 1880s they decided to push into the interior of Mali to build a railroad across the Sahara. To do this, they had to overcome the armies of Ahmadu Tall and Samory Touré. Both surrendered to French forces by the 1890s, while the Tuareg kept fighting French rule.

A young French colonel, T.P.E. Bonnier, believed Timbuktu was strategic because of its location at the northern curve of the Niger River. He developed a two-pronged attack—by river and by land. Bonnier directed the river attack himself and reached Timbuktu without much resistance on January 10, 1894. But five days later, Tuareg warriors killed Bonnier and 11 of his officers in a surprise attack.

Meanwhile, General Joseph Joffre arrived with 400 troops on February 12, 1894, after covering a distance of 508 miles. The French defeated the Tuareg and took over Timbuktu. Southwest of the city, Joffre immediately began building Fort Bonnier, which was near the river so pirogues could be sent to Kabara, where the French navy docked its gunboats. By 1900 the French flag was flying in Timbuktu and throughout Mali.

When the French occupied Timbuktu, they raised their tricolor flag, unnecessarily provoking the Tuareg.

Tuareg at War

The Tuareg were masters of guerrilla warfare, especially at night. As an enemy force advanced, they captured any straying soldiers. Sentinels on camels watched from sand dunes, while slaves, armed with lances, hid behind bushes. Directing the action were the chiefs on horseback. Before a battle, griots [singer-poets] chanted battle songs to excite the Tuareg warriors.

FORT BONNIER

White Monk

The ex-priest known as Père Yakouba of France became legendary as the "white monk of Timbuktu." Giving up his orders as a member of the clergy, he married a local woman named Salama, had children with her, and lived as one of Timbuktu's leading citizens.

A Colonial City

By the 1940s, Timbuktu was a city of uneasy peace. The still-hostile Tuareg were under the thumb of the French. Protected by forts run by French officers and 700 local soldiers, a European's life was safe. "On the other hand," wrote anthropologist Horace Miner, "an admired resident of the city is the son of an Arab who murdered the French commander some years ago."

After 45 years of French rule, life was fairly stable and yet marked by tensions—between colonist and resident and between urban dweller and nomad. Three languages were spoken—Songhai, Arabic, and Tuareg. The city was divided into four quarters. Streets in Timbuktu were narrow and bordered by the walls of houses. There were no city blocks because the walls were continuous except for doorways. And there was no room for a car until mid-century, when the French tore down houses to widen a few streets.

Outside Timbuktu small dwellings were clustered together. Grass thatch was laid over a frame of wood, 6 to 8 feet high at the center and 15 feet wide. The houses had no windows and only one low doorway. A fire could not be built inside, so the cooking was done outside.

Racing camels, called *meharis*, marched in front of Fort Bonnier in 1941.

Family Matters

Family life in Timbuktu during the colonial period began at sunrise. Children usually woke up first and then roused their parents with a greeting. In Arab families, the husband and wife prayed together every morning. They ate with their children out of a common bowl, but teenagers were not allowed to talk during the meal. Boys left the house early and went out to greet grandparents, uncles, and aunts.

Although most Songhai families were involved in some form of trade, they believed that relatives were more valuable than money. Husbands wanted their wives to have many children, partly because they believed that the more children they had, the more people would honor them after their death.

Changes in Family Discipline

Up until the French colonial period, family councils called qadis handled even serious crimes, such as murder and robbery. In the old days, if teenage brothers and sisters were caught fighting, they would be whipped in front of the family council. Young girls were taken to parties, but the boys were not allowed to go out until they had turned 15. If a relative saw a boy running loose, they spanked him and sent him home.

Timbuktu's extended families were closely knit, and the father was a stern influence. Local people believed that large, close family units "kept something from coming between you and your brother."

According to this belief, a man shared his children with his brother. Sometimes a richer brother adopted one or two of a poorer brother's children and raised them as his own. Aunts and uncles taught children the local lifeways. A girl learned how to dress and fix her hair from her aunt. Nephews learned about religious and social values from an uncle.

When family arguments arose, the oldest family member, or patriarch, called a family council to settle the conflict. If one family member had actually hurt another, the patriarch might offer to pay the injured party to bring peace. If a family member continued to disobey the family council or to cause problems, he or she could be cast out of the family.

49

Food and Health

Salt continued to be Timbuktu's most important item of trade. In fact, the central market had moved farther north in the city, away from the river, to signify the importance of meeting the two annual salt caravans that came from Taou-denni.

Most of Timbuktu's food still had to be brought in because the city grew very little of its own. Typical foodstuffs included wheat, shea butter, sugared tea, peppers, garlic, pimentos, milk, poultry, goat meat, and wheat bread. Kola nuts were more important than vegetables because they didn't perish in the heat.

Farmers along the river grew rice, millet, and a type of sorghum called guinea corn. When the rains stopped,

Learning to cook

grain was hoarded. Even when the rains returned, merchants held back grain to raise prices.

Although Timbuktu was part of the French colonial empire, its people experienced sicknesses that doctors in France had already learned to relieve. Malaria, sleeping sickness, eye infections that could cause blindness, tropical ulcers, pneumonia, amoebic dysentery, tuberculosis, syphilis, meningitis, mumps, and trachoma took their toll on the population. Cholera had been checked, but cases of leprosy still broke out. In the mid-twentieth century, the life expectancy of someone living in Timbuktu was only 41.

Pounding millet

Dress in Timbuktu

The streets of colonial Timbuktu reflected the diversity of the local population. Different cultural groups could be distinguished on the basis of clothes, jewelry, and hairstyle. Women tended to wear a brightly colored outer robe draped around the body and over the head. Although most of the residents were Muslims—and Islamic law encouraged women to wear veils—Timbuktu's women usually did not. Arab women, though, on entering the street, tended to draw the end of their robe over their faces. All of the women wore jewelry, including rings of silver and stone, necklaces of gold, amber or shell, heavy C-shaped bracelets of silver and ebony or beads, plus a great variety of earrings. Even nursing babies wore bracelets and anklets. Girl babies had pieces of yarn threaded through pierced earlobes.

Men also wore loose robes, which covered roomy pantaloons. Tuareg men continued to wear veils. They also wore stone bracelets on their arms that never came off. Most men wore sandals or locally made slippers.

Parents shaved a boy's or a girl's head when the baby was only a week old. Each family in the different ethnic groups had its own design for leaving a small tuft of hair. The reason behind the tufted hair design was explained in a story. At death adults were required to climb a treacherous mountain ridge to reach paradise. If their deeds had been good, they would make it to the top. If they had committed too many wrongs, they would fall off the ridge and never reach paradise. Children, however, were not under these rules. A child who died also had to climb the ridge but had two angels as helpers. If by accident the child happened to fall off the ridge, the angels could grab the child by the tuft of hair and carry the child to paradise.

The local well has long been a gathering place for Timbuktu's women. In the early morning they gather water. Midmorning is bath time for the children.

Timbuktu after Independence

During World War II (1939–1945), France and other countries fought Germany, which temporarily took over France. Soldiers from Timbuktu and other parts of Mali helped the leading French general, Charles de Gaulle, fight back. Soon after the war ended, de Gaulle became president of France. He rewarded the Malian people with more freedom. By 1960 Mali had achieved full independence as the Republic of Mali. Among the new republic's challenges was coping with drought and with outbreaks of violence among the peoples in and around Timbuktu.

Timbuktu's fate has always depended on the rise and fall of the Niger River. Because of a very long period of drought, the river is rising later each year, delaying the arrival of the transport boats. Merchants sit in their mud houses, waiting for business. As one Timbuktu official put it, "Ten years ago, the first boat arrived on July 1. Now we're lucky [if] it's here by early August. In another five years, who knows?"

Timbuktu has also had struggles with a changing citizenry. In 1990 a group of radical Tuareg joined with Libya in an unsuccessful rebellion against the government of Mali. Thousands of Tuareg were forced to abandon their animals and flee, many finding refuge outside of Timbuktu. In 1992 a peace treaty was signed, granting the Tuareg the freedom to return to the desert. Drought, property loss, and the possibility of education for their children are all factors that have encouraged people to remain in Timbuktu.

55

Kids in Timbuktu

C hildren in Timbuktu have little time to play. Boys begin school with an intense study of the Koran that often lasts several years. Boys must also attend a more standard school where they learn geography, reading, writing, and foreign languages.

After school, they might race toy vehicles carved of wood or play games with their friends. Boys also have many chores, often caring for family animals or helping their father in his labor.

Girls have a somewhat different daily routine. As women in Timbuktu are primarily housewives, girls are taught at an early age to weave, cook, and clean. Girls often have chores such as gathering well water and buying family necessities in the market. They balance packages on the top of their heads, allowing their whole body to bear the weight. They also care for their younger siblings and cousins. Girls attend school, as well, although their religious studies are less involved.

The government of Mali struggles to provide the country's children with education and health-care services.

Visiting Timbuktu

*T*hese days people visit Timbuktu to be able to say they've been to a place once considered to lie at the end of the world. Despite a decrease in population and wealth and damage to its historic buildings, Timbuktu is still remembered for its past glories. But the decay has been severe. "Timbuktu has been losing its vitality steadily for the past 500 years," said recent visitor Joshua Hammer. It sometimes seems that Timbuktu's greatest source of income is postage. Everyone who visits wants to send a postcard from the local post office, stamped with the date and the world-famous name "Timbuktu."

Yet Timbuktu has more to rely on than its famous name. In recent times, citizens have enjoyed a resurgence of interest in the city's academic past. In 1976 a research center was founded in Timbuktu, called the Centre de Documentation et de Recherches Ahmad Baba (CEDRAB). By the late 1990s, the center had collected almost 6,000 historical documents in Arabic.

Despite waning tourism and persistent drought, Timbuktu has survived for more than 800 years. People in the area are learning to put to work their ancient knowledge of farming, fishing, and raising livestock. The government of Mali is promoting small-scale projects, rather than large-scale industrial ones, to encourage local initiative. Timbuktu may once again emerge as a shining pearl on the edge of a great river.

The trading traditions of this famous city linger on in the outdoor markets that still thrive in modern-day Timbuktu.

Timbuktu Timeline

40,000 B.C.–A.D. 1330 Origins	**40,000 B.C.**	Ancient *Homo sapiens* hunt elephants and lions in the forests of what would become the Sahara Desert. They catch fish in the large lakes.
	A.D. 640	Muslim armies enter Africa
	A.D. 1009	King of Songhai people accepts the religon of Islam
	A.D. 1076	Ghana Empire falls
	A.D. 1100	Tuareg settlers camp along the Niger River. The camping area becomes Timbuktu.
	A.D. 1312	Mansa Musa becomes king of Mali
	A.D. 1324	Mansa Musa makes a pilgrimage to Mecca
A.D. 1330-1591 Golden Age	**A.D. 1330**	Mansa Musa returns to Timbuktu with Al-Saheli, an architect, who builds a palace and a large mosque
	A.D. 1353	Ibn Battutah, a Moroccan traveler, visits Timbuktu and describes its wealth and security
	A.D. 1375	Abraham Cresques creates the earliest map of West Africa that shows Timbuktu
	A.D. 1433	The Tuareg capture Timbuktu
	A.D. 1464	Sonni Ali becomes king of Songhai
	A.D. 1468	Sonni Ali captures Timbuktu
	A.D. 1492	Sonni Ali dies
	A.D. 1493	Askia Muhammad comes to power and rebuilds Timbuktu to its greatest height as a center of trade and Islamic scholarship
	A.D. 1510	Leo Africanus visits Timbuktu and describes it as an exceedingly rich city

A.D. 1591-1805 **Decline and Rebirth**	**A.D. 1591**	Moroccan army crosses the Sahara and seizes Timbuktu, burning most of its libraries
A.D. 1805–1960 **Colonization**	**A.D. 1805**	Mungo Park becomes first European to visit Timbuktu
	A.D. 1826	Alexander Gordon Laing travels to Timbuktu but is murdered on his way back to Europe
	A.D. 1828	René-August Caillié arrives in Timbuktu and lives to tell his story
	A.D. 1894	French gunboats sail up the Niger River and take over Timbuktu. A small French army, traveling through the desert, arrives soon afterward. France annexes most of the region.
A.D. 1960-present **Modern Timbuktu**	**A.D. 1960**	Mali gains independence. Timbuktu becomes part of the new Republic of Mali.
	A.D. 1970s	Severe drought destroys the nomadic lifestyle of many Tuareg
	A.D. 1980s	War occurs between the Tuareg and armies from Mali, Burkina Faso, Mauritania, and Niger
	A.D. 1992	The government of Mali and the Tuareg coalition sign a peace agreement
	A.D. 1990s	Tourists and scholars continue to visit Timbuktu

Pronunciation Guide

Djenné	jeh-NAY	*qadis*	kah-DEES
Djinguerber	jihn-gwehr-BEHR	*René-Auguste Caillié*	ruh-NAY–aw-GOOST KY-YAY
harquebuses	HAAHR-kwih-behs-ehs		
Ibn Battutah	ihb-ehn baht-TOO-tah	*Taou-denni*	tahoo-deh-NAY
mirabouts	mih-rah-BOO	*Tuareg*	TWAH-rehg

Books about Mali and Timbuktu

Arnold, Caroline. *Camel.* New York: Morrow Junior Books, 1992.

Dobler, Lavinia and William A. Brown. *Great Rulers of the African Past.* Garden City, NY: Doubleday, 1965.

Goodsmith, Lauren. *Children of Mauritania: Days in the Desert and by the River Shore.* Minneapolis: Carolrhoda Books, Inc., 1993.

Haskins, Jim and Joann Biundi. *From Afar to Zulu: A Dictionary of African Cultures.* New York: Walker and Company, 1995.

Jenkins, Martin. *Deserts (Endangered People and Places).* Minneapolis: Lerner Publications Company, 1995.

Koslow, Philip. *Mali: Crossroads of Africa.* New York: Chelsea House Publishers, 1995.

Mann, Kenny. *Ghana, Mali, Songhay: The Western Sudan. African Kingdoms of the Past.* Parsippany, NJ: Dillon Press, 1996.

McKissack, Patricia and Frederick McKissack. *The Royal Kingdoms of Ghana, Mali and Songhay: Life In Medieval Africa.* New York: Henry Holt and Company, 1994.

Niane, D. T. *Sundiata: An Epic of Old Mali.* Translated by G. D. Pickett. White Plains, NY: Longman, 1960.

O'Toole, Thomas. *Mali In Pictures (Visual Geography Series).* Minneapolis: Lerner Publications Company, 1996.

Reynolds, Jan. *Sahara (Vanishing Cultures).* San Diego: Harcourt Brace Jovanovich, 1991.

Rochegude, Anne. *Tarlift, Tuareg Boy: My Village in the Sahara.* Translated and adapted by Bridget Daly. Morristown, NJ: Silver Burdett, 1985.

Steele, Philip. *Deserts (Geography Detective).* Minneapolis: Carolrhoda Books, Inc., 1996.

Index

About the Author and Illustrator

Larry Brook grew up in Cameroon, West Africa, and speaks French and Bulu, a West African language. He has traveled widely throughout the world as a facilitator of writing and leadership training courses. He is married, lives in Elgin, Illinois, and has three daughters. He is fascinated by varied human cultures, both ancient and modern. This is his first children's book.

Ray Webb of Woodstock, England, studied art and design at Birmingham Polytechnic in Birmingham, England. A specialist in historical and scientific subjects, his work has been published in Great Britain, the Netherlands, Germany, and the United States. He continues to teach and lecture and especially enjoys introducing young people to illustration as a career opportunity.

Acknowledgments

For quoted material: p. 4, *New York Times International,* 30 January 1995; p. 9, Horace Miner. *The Primitive City of Timbuctu* (Princeton, NJ: Princeton University Press, 1953); p. 11, Warren J. Halliburton. *Nomads of the Sahara* (New York: Crestwood House, 1992); p. 16, Galbraith Welch. *Africa Before They Came* (New York: William Morrow, 1965); p. 19, Welch. *Africa Before;* p. 19, J. F. A. Ajayi and Michael Crowder. *History of West Africa.* Vol. I (Harlow Essex, UK: Longman Group Ltd., 1971); p. 24, Jefferson E. Murphy. *History of African Civilization: The Peoples, Nations, Kingdoms, and Empires of Africa from Prehistory to the Present* (New York: Thomas Crowell Co., 1972); pp. 26–27, Kenny Mann. *African Kingdoms of the Past: Ghana, Mali, Songhay, the Western Sudan.* (Parsippany, NJ: Dillon Press, 1996); p. 31, Murphy, *History of African Civilization;* p. 32, Lester Brooks. *Great Civilizations of Ancient Africa* (New York: Four Winds Press, 1971); p. 34, L.H. Ofosu-Appiah. *People in Bondage* (Minneapolis: Runestone Press, 1993); pp. 40–41, René-Auguste Caillié. *Travels Through Central Africa to Timbuctoo.* Vol. I. and Vol. II (London: Frank Cass, 1968); p. 47, Miner. *Primitive City;* pp. 55, 58, Joshua Hammer. "Still Here," *New Republic,* 13 November 1995.

For photographs and art reproductions: CHE18163 Cheltenham Art Gallery & Museums, Gloucestershire/UK/Bridgeman Art Library, London/New York, pp. 6–7; Musée d'Orsay, Paris/ET Archive, London/SuperStock, pp. 12–13; Private Collection/Beth Hinckley/SuperStock, pp. 14–15; Christie's Images/SuperStock, pp. 16–17, 42–43; The Granger Collection, New York, pp. 24–25, 39 (inset); North Wind Picture Archives, pp. 28–29, 33; Gladys J. Peterson, pp. 28–29 (insets), 54–55, 56, 57, 58–59; The Lowe Art Museum, University of Miami/SuperStock, p. 33 (inset); Stock Montage, Inc., p. 35; Tretiakov Gallery, Moscow, Russia/SuperStock, p. 36; Historical Pictures/Stock Montage, pp. 38–39; Mary Evans Picture Library, pp. 40–41, 44–45; © Field Museum, Chicago, IL Neg. #Z79295, pp. 46–47. Cover: Independent Picture Service.